GOLDEN RETRIEVERS

FAVORITE DOG BREEDS

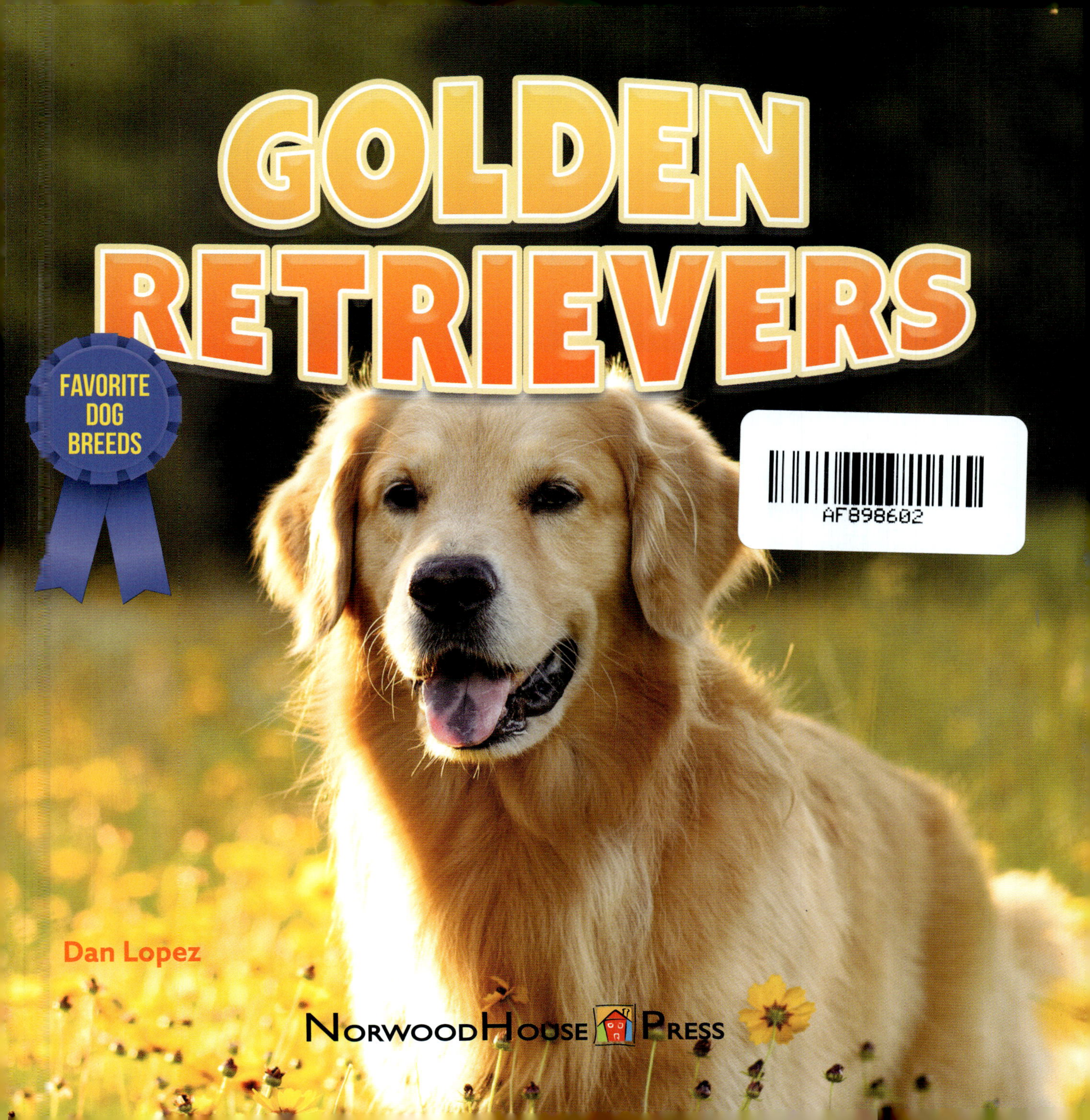

Dan Lopez

NorwoodHouse Press

Cataloging-in-Publication Data

Names: Lopez, Dan.
Title: Golden retrievers / Dan Lopez.
Description: Buffalo, NY : Norwood House Press, 2027. | Series: Favorite dog breeds | Includes glossary and index.
Identifiers: ISBN 9781978580299 (pbk.) | ISBN 9781978580305 (library bound) | ISBN 9781978580312 (ebook)
Subjects: LCSH: Golden retriever--Juvenile literature. | Dog breeds--Juvenile literature.
Classification: LCC SF429.G63 L67 2027 | DDC 636.7527--dc23

Published in 2027 by
Norwood House Press
2544 Clinton Street
Buffalo, NY 14224

Designer: Rhea Magaro
Editor: Tricia Hoffman

Photo credits: Cover, pp.1, 5 Tanya Consaul Photography/Shutterstock.com; p.4 Wikipedia; p.7 BESTWEB/Shutterstock.com; p.8 Eric Isselee/Shutterstock.com; p.9 Kev Gregory/Shutterstock.com; p.11 TravelGirl1981/Shutterstock.com; p.12 Wildpix 645/Shutterstock.com; p.13 BRS images/Shutterstock.com; p.15 Saley Yanny/Shutterstock.com; p.16 SasaStock/Shutterstock.com; p.17 Monkey Business Images/Shutterstock.com; p.19 Rzytalke/Shutterstock.com; p.21 Alina Ziabrieva/Shutterstock.com;

Printed in the United States of America

CPSIA compliance information: Batch #CSNHP27: For further information contact Norwood House Press at 1-800-237-9932.

TABLE OF CONTENTS

Meet the Golden Retriever

Golden retrievers are popular pets. Dogs of this **breed** are known for having beautiful, golden-brown **coats**. They are gentle and friendly.

The star of the *Air Bud* movies is a golden retriever.

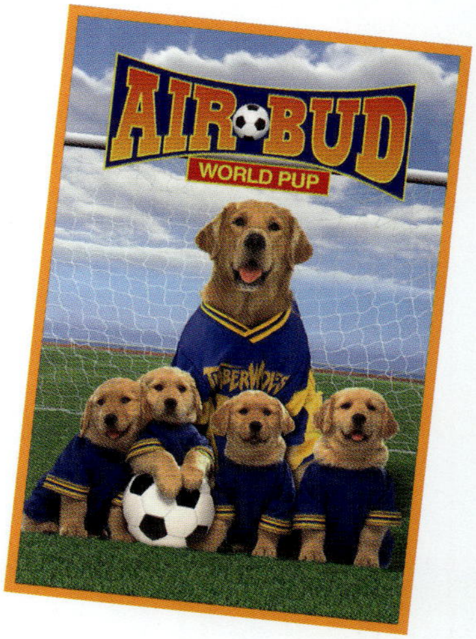

What Do Golden Retrievers Look Like?

Golden retrievers are medium-to-large dogs. They can stand 24 inches (61 centimeters) tall. They can weigh up to 75 pounds (34 kilograms).

These **muscular** dogs have wide heads with straight **muzzles**. Their short ears flop forward.

A golden retriever's honey-colored fur grows long and feathery on its neck, legs, and tail.

Where Do Golden Retrievers Come From?

Hunters in Scotland first bred golden retrievers in the 1800s. They wanted dogs that could stand up to the country's rugged mountains and lakes.

Golden retrievers were bred to **retrieve** ducks and other **waterfowl**. They like to carry things in their mouths. Some can even carry an egg without breaking it!

Golden retrievers are excellent swimmers. They have webbed feet. Their heavy fur is **water-repellent**.

Do Golden Retrievers Make Good Pets?

Golden retrievers are **easygoing**. They are trusting and **affectionate**. These animals get along with people and with other dogs. They make great family pets.

Golden retrievers are smart and hardworking. They can be trained to work as guide dogs for people who are blind. Police officers use them to find missing people.

Golden retrievers make good **therapy dogs**. They bring a sense of calm and happiness to schools, hospitals, and nursing homes.

What Do Golden Retrievers Need?

Golden retrievers are strong and full of energy. They need plenty of exercise.

Active play keeps them healthy and happy. They love to play fetch. They love to swim!

Golden retrievers are big eaters! Owners must be careful not to feed them too much.

Their thick coats can shed. These dogs need to be brushed a few times each week.

Glossary

affectionate (uh-FEK-shuh-nit): loving and caring

breed (breed): one type or kind of an animal

coats (kohts): the hair or fur that covers animals' bodies

easygoing (ee-zee-GOH-ing): relaxed and carefree; not stressed out

muscular (MUHS-kyuh-lur): having strong muscles

muzzles (MUHZ-uhlz): the parts of animal faces that include the nose and mouth; snouts

retrieve (ri-TREEVE): to get something and bring it back; dogs that are retrievers find and bring back animals shot by hunters

therapy dogs (THER-uh-pee dawgz): dogs that work in the community to keep people company, reduce their stress, help them do exercises, and help them learn new things

waterfowl (WAW-tur-foul): birds that live near water, such as ducks and geese

water-repellent (WAW-tur-ri-PEL-unt): resists water, but not completely waterproof

Thinking Questions

1. Describe a golden retriever's coat.
2. Describe a golden retriever's personality.
3. What were golden retrievers bred to do?
4. What kinds of outdoor activities do golden retrievers like?
5. Why do golden retrievers make good therapy dogs?

Index

About the Author

Dan Lopez is a writer who loves dogs! He has a German shepherd named Hans and an Irish setter named Tam. They love to go for walks in the woods together. Sometimes, they jump in the lake for a swim. Dan lives in Indiana with his wife and three kids.